Disasters in Nature

Earthquakes

Catherine Chambers

Heinemann Library
Chicago, Illinois

© 2001 Reed Educational & Professional Publishing
Published by Heinemann Library,
an imprint of Reed Educational & Professional Publishing,
100 N. LaSalle, Suite 1010
Chicago, IL 60602
Customer Service 888-454-2279
Visit our website at www.heinemannlibrary.com

Designed by Celia Floyd
Originated by Dot Gradations
Printed by Wing King Tong, in Hong Kong

05 04 03 02 01
10 9 8 7 6 5 4 3 2 1

Library of Congress Cataloging-in-Publication Data

Chambers, Catherine, 1954-
　　Earthquakes / Catherine Chambers.
　　　　p. cm. — (Disasters in nature)
　　Includes bibliographical references and index.
　　Summary: Examines earthquakes, discussing what causes them, how they are measured, and how they can cause tsunamis. Includes a section on the San Francisco earthquake of 1989.
　　ISBN 1-57572-427-8 (lib. bdg.)
　　1. Earthquakes—Juvenile literature. [1. Earthquakes.] I. Title.

QE521.3.C452 2000
551.22—dc21

00-020026

Acknowledgments

The Publishers would like to thank the following for permission to reproduce photographs:

Magnum Photos/Susan Meiselas, p. 5; Rex Features, pp. 7, 11, 34, 37, 44, 45; Popperfoto, p. 9; FLPA/Mark Newman, p. 15; Tony Stone/Deborah Davis, p. 16; Camera Press/Itar-Tass Photo Agency, p. 17; FLPA/S. McCutcheon, pp. 18, 25; Mary Evans, p. 19; Corbis/Vince Streano, p. 22; Tony Stone/Bob Thomas, p. 27; Science Photo Library/NASA, p. 29; Tony Stone/Thomas Brase, p. 31; Corbis, p. 32; Corbis/Tony Arruza, p. 38; Photri, pp. 39, 41; FLPA/D.P. Wilson, p. 40; Magnum Photos/George Rodger, p. 43.

Cover photograph reproduced with permission of Robert Harding Picture Library.

Our thanks to Matthew Slagel of the University of Chicago for his comments in the preparation of this book.

Every effort has been made to contact copyright holders of any material reproduced in this book. Any omissions will be rectified in subsequent printings if notice is given to the Publisher.

Some words are shown in bold, **like this.** You can find out what they mean by looking in the glossary.

Contents

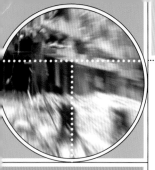

Introduction

What is an Earthquake?

The earth's surface is constantly shifting. When the ground beneath us moves, it usually does it so slowly that we do not notice. Sometimes, however, it moves with a huge force—sliding, slipping, shaking, sinking—that it becomes very noticeable! This is called an earthquake. There are thousands of earthquakes on the earth's surface each year, and there are many others deep in the earth's crust that we do not feel. Some of these are measured by sensitive instruments called **seismometers,** so we know that they occur. Out of about 3,000 earthquakes that we sense on the surface each year, only a few will cause disasters.

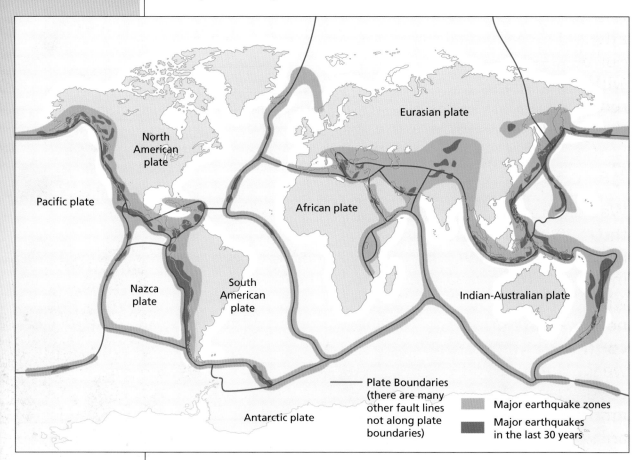

Eurasian plate

North American plate

Pacific plate

African plate

Nazca plate

South American plate

Indian-Australian plate

Antarctic plate

——— Plate Boundaries (there are many other fault lines not along plate boundaries)

Major earthquake zones

Major earthquakes in the last 30 years

This map shows how earthquake activity is related to the fault lines that separate the earth's tectonic plates. However, an earthquake that begins on a fault line can cause tremors that affect the surface hundreds of miles away.

Where do earthquakes happen?

The earth's crust is made of enormous **tectonic plates** that are pushing together or pulling apart all the time. Under the oceans, hot, sticky rock oozes from under the earth's crust, creating ridges and mountains along the edges of the plates. As the edges of the plates grate together or slip and slide, they cause the earth to tremble. The areas of the world that are most often affected are China, Japan, and other western Pacific islands, the west coast of the Americas, central Asia, and the Mediterranean.

Earthquakes in our hands

It is far too late to keep people from living in areas affected by earthquakes, but we can try to construct our buildings, bridges, roads, and railroads so that they withstand most of the shock. We can also try to reduce the problems after the earthquake—the fires that rage and the services that grind to a halt.

Earthquakes on our minds

We hear about earthquake disasters regularly through the media, but we hear more quickly about disasters in some areas than others. Some earthquakes happen in very remote areas, or poor parts of the world where road networks and other **communications** are weak. This means that governments and international aid agencies are slow to react. Relief efforts are hindered because getting to the affected communities is difficult.

Mexico City's millions of citizens were totally unprepared for the earthquake disaster that struck on September 19, 1985. The disaster claimed about 10,000 lives.

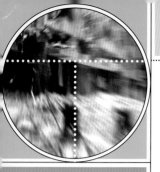

San Francisco—an Earthquake Disaster

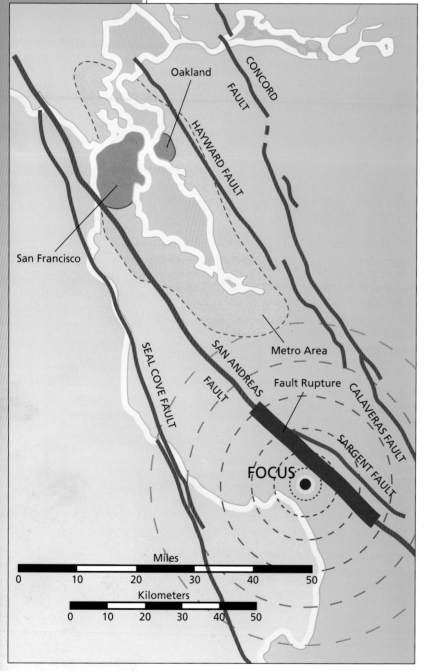

Oakland

CONCORD FAULT

HAYWARD FAULT

San Francisco

SEAL COVE FAULT

SAN ANDREAS FAULT

Metro Area

Fault Rupture

CALAVERAS FAULT

SARGENT FAULT

FOCUS

Miles
0   10   20   30   40   50

Kilometers
0   10   20   30   40   50

The San Andreas Fault is about 660 miles (1050 kilometers) long. The 1989 earthquake displaced a section of a 269-mile (430-kilometer) rift made during the devastating tremor that hit San Francisco in 1906.

About 60 miles (96 kilometers) south of San Francisco, at 5:04 P.M. on October 17, 1989, a section of the San Andreas fault system slipped. Part of the Loma Prieta Peak in the Santa Cruz mountains suddenly lurched 6 feet (2 meters) northward. A 25-mile (40-kilometer) section of the fault was displaced. Just six seconds later **seismic waves** hit San Francisco Bay to the north. For 15 long seconds the ground shook. Buildings tumbled, electricity cables and gas pipes were severed, and fires broke out. Roads and bridges collapsed. Sixty-eight people were killed and 3,757 were injured. The emergency services were stretched to their limits.

How did it happen?

The San Andreas fault line separates the North American and Pacific **tectonic plates,** running all the way from northwest California to the Gulf of California. For several days before the earthquake, a lot of small tremors had been registered in the area and scientists believed that a "big one" was due. The plates normally slide past each other quite smoothly, causing only faint tremors, but there are some parts that jam against each other as they slide, building up stresses that are eventually released as an earthquake. This is exactly what happened on October 17. The 15-second quake reached 7.1 on the **Richter Scale,** which is very high.

Where did the damage occur?

Most of the damage occurred in the Marina District near the coast. The buildings worst affected were those built on soft ground, such as floodplains—flat areas of land surrounding wide rivers. Landfill sites were also badly hit. These areas were once lagoons—coastal inlets of water protected by raised sandbanks. The lagoons had been filled in with rubble and then built upon. As the earth vibrated, the soft, loose ground began to move around like a liquid, making the buildings on top of it sink or shake even more. This is known as the **liquefaction** effect.

The San Francisco earthquake of 1989 destroyed 1,018 homes and damaged 23,408.

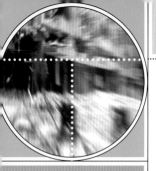

After the Disaster

Who paid for the damage?

It took a long time for San Francisco's politicians to fund the repairs to **infrastructures** such as roads and bridges. Immediate repairs often have to be paid for with money borrowed from banks and other financial institutions, which charge interest on the loans. This means that the borrower has to pay back a lot more money than the repair job actually cost.

Many homes and businesses claimed repair money through their **insurance policies,** but not everyone had not taken out insurance. Some had policies that did not cover damage done by earthquakes. The problem of who pays for repairs is a difficult one. The United States suffers a huge range of natural disasters—hurricanes, tornadoes, floods, drought, earthquakes, and even volcanoes. In some parts of the country it simply costs too much to be insured against natural disasters at all.

Waiting for the next one

When the San Andreas fault was inspected, it was found that the displacement had occurred on the southernmost part of the fault that had caused a major earthquake in 1906. This previous quake had destroyed half of the city. It had taken 83 years for pressure to build up from this "locked" section of the San Andreas fault and be released as an earthquake. This same fracture—although not exactly the same **epicenter**—with its identical "hit" on San Francisco was the starting point for scientists trying to work out when the next "big one" would occur. The task now is to examine the forces put upon the mountains by the same clash of **tectonic plates** and to try to estimate how long it will take for pressure to build up again.

Pressure points

- In the year following the disaster, 7,000 more shocks—not all felt by humans—were recorded in the San Francisco area.

- Five of the shocks measured more than 5.0 on the **Richter Scale,** and 40 measured more than 4.0.

Aid and arguments

It often takes a disaster like this to show the real needs of a city and to get people to take action. The emergency services responded quickly and efficiently to the San Francisco earthquake. However, lack of resources made their work difficult. In February 1990, the San Francisco Firefighters' Union mounted a protest at budget cuts that had kept them from effectively tackling the fires following the earthquake, and from rescuing people trapped by fallen buildings. The firefighters presented 70,000 signatures to the Registrar of Voters to show how many people supported their plea for more resources. The President of the union said, "The havoc it [the earthquake] wrought showed just how thin our forces have been spread since the budget cuts."

After the 1906 earthquake in San Francisco, a lot of thought went into rebuilding the city. Research and development into specialized earthquake-resistant architecture had taken place not only in the United States but also in other earthquake zones, especially Japan.

9

Hitting the Headlines

Which earthquakes make the headlines? Why do some parts of the world get more media attention than others? And why is too much coverage not always appreciated?

Positive and negative

Pictures of the San Francisco earthquake were soon televised by satellite around the world. These images attracted the attention of millions of people and prompted many offers of assistance, which continued well into the following year. In February 1990, Taipei, Taiwan—San Francisco's sister city—donated $100,000 to the earthquake disaster fund. Taipei itself lies in an earthquake zone, so its people were sympathetic.

A month earlier, and only three months after the disaster, business leaders had been complaining that worldwide coverage of the earthquake had projected an image of total devastation. Pictures of rubble and burning buildings made it look as if the whole city had gone up in smoke. The tourist industry had been especially badly affected. This led the spokeswoman for the Convention and Visitors' Bureau to plead for the promotion of a more positive image of the city. She pointed out that the area worst affected was the Marina district—not the Wharf, where visitors could still receive the highest standards of hospitality.

Choosing stories

Why is it that one earthquake may make headlines, while another similar one is ignored? Some earthquakes occur in remote areas, where roads and **communication** networks are bad. Journalists and aid agencies find it difficult to reach the disaster zone in areas like these. Also, some governments may not want to attract the attention of the outside world, so they try to cope alone. This is what happened in Tangshan, China, in 1976.

Worldwide, what happens in some countries is reported more carefully than what goes on in others. A superpower such as the United States is watched by the rest of the world all the time. Foreign media networks have journalists posted permanently in Washington, D.C. The excellent transportation and communication networks in the United States enable camera crews to reach a disaster zone very quickly once an earthquake hits.

The earthquake that struck Tangshan city in China on July 28, 1976 was so violent that people were thrown 6 feet (2 meters) into the air. Altogether, over 230,000 people lost their lives. But at that time, China's government was not popular in many parts of the world, especially in the United States and western Europe, so this particular earthquake was never fully reported by the international media.

Waves Beneath our Feet

Earthquakes occur mostly along the lines where the earth's crust divides into huge masses of land called **tectonic plates.** The plates shift at a rate of a few inches (several centimeters) each year. They do not always glide smoothly past each other. Sometimes they suddenly catch and then break free, creating **seismic waves** that rise to the surface. Several thousand of these are felt as earthquakes above ground every year, while thousands more go undetected. Earthquakes also occur at fault lines, where a fault plane meets the surface. These fault lines do not have to be at a split between two plates, but some are.

Fault lines do not extend all the way around a tectonic plate. They tend to form jagged lines, from smaller sections of rifts or tears, that are not always connected. The San Francisco earthquake of 1989 was caused by a sudden movement along just a section of the San Andreas Fault, not along its whole length. Sometimes, parts of the fault get stuck, and the pressure builds up for many years until the rock finally gives way.

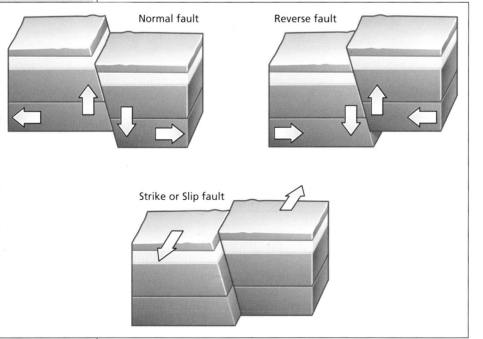

Normal fault

Reverse fault

Strike or Slip fault

Some faults slip down, some are thrust upwards, while others slide along each other without moving up or down at all.

How the fault shifts

The huge forces created by a moving fault bend the rock on either side. When the strain is too great, the force is released in seismic waves and sudden movement occurs along the fault. This relieves the pressure on the earth's crust, and the rocks, although cracked, are no longer strained—just displaced.

The movement begins deep down at a point called the **focus,** sometimes called the hypocenter. The point on the surface directly above the focus is called the **epicenter.** Seismic waves spread out from the focus and the epicenter. The epicenter refracts them along the surface. Tremors are felt when these seismic waves reach new areas.

Where the earth moves

Near the surface, the earth's crust is cold and brittle, so it can be damaged by powerful seismic waves. But under the crust is a hot, supple layer, called the **mantle,** which is wrapped around the core of the earth. Because it is so hot, it behaves like a soft material. The tectonic plates move around slowly on top of the mantle all the time. Some earthquakes occur where the plates buckle or break. Most earthquakes, and the largest, occur around the earth's **subduction zones.** These are where one plate dips below another, into the mantle, as we can see in the diagram.

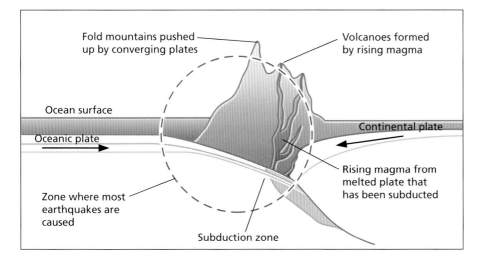

Fold mountains pushed up by converging plates

Volcanoes formed by rising magma

Ocean surface

Continental plate

Oceanic plate

Rising magma from melted plate that has been subducted

Zone where most earthquakes are caused

Subduction zone

Earthquakes occur where one plate slips down under the other. Molten rock is generated as the bottom crust is heated by the earth's mantle.

What's in a Wave?

The waves of energy that make the earth tremble and crack are called **seismic waves.** "Seismic" comes from a Greek word meaning "to shake." Each wave has its own **frequency,** which can be determined by counting the number of waves that pass the same point within a certain time. Each wave can have a different height, or **amplitude.** Seismic waves are not all the same—they make different patterns as they move. All these things give waves their own characteristics and tell us the kind of impact they will make. One of the most important things that affect the way seismic waves move is the material through which they pass.

All seismic waves travel faster and maintain a regular pattern when they move through very hard uniform material, such as **granite** rock. Soft materials such as soil and river **sediment** have a less rigid and more varied texture. This means that waves travel more slowly and are more easily disrupted.

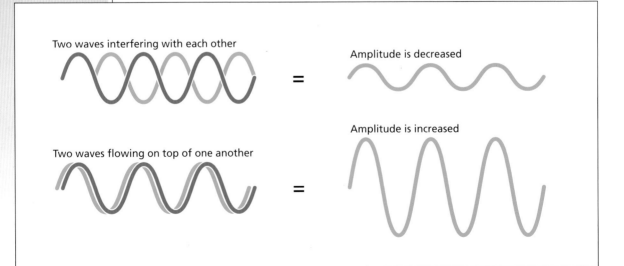

Two waves interfering with each other

Amplitude is decreased

Amplitude is increased

Two waves flowing on top of one another

Wave interference can have different effects on the strength of an earthquake. When two waves move together, their amplitude is increased and the quake will be stronger. But when a peak of one wave meets the trough of another, the waves interfere with each other. This decreases their amplitude.

Making patterns

The two main types of seismic waves are **body waves** and **surface waves.** Body waves move through bodies of solid rock. There are two different types of body waves—**pressure waves** and **shear waves.** Pressure waves vibrate lengthways through the material, in the direction the wave is traveling. Shear waves vibrate at right angles to their direction of travel.

Surface waves move along the rock surfaces or layers of different types of rocks. Because the different waves move at different speeds, **seismologists** can measure and compare their speed and direction. Using this information, they can then calculate an earthquake's **epicenter** and **focus.**

Energy waves would have a difficult journey through this rock, which has many layers of different types, textures, and densities.

Pressure points

- Seismic waves are most damaging when they come from a shallow **focus** less than 18 miles (30 kilometers) beneath the earth's surface.

- The next most damaging occur from a medium depth of 30–50 miles (50–80 kilometers).

- The least damaging are those rippling from a deep focus, more than 50 miles (80 kilometers) beneath the earth's surface.

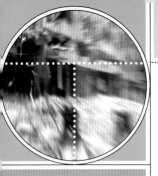

Moving the Earth

Sections of the earth's crust move all the time. While scientists can measure the few inches that they shift each year, most of us cannot see where movement is occurring. This type of movement is known as **fault creep.** There are few signs of it on the surface because the energy waves are too slow and weak, but sudden fault movement causes violent waves of energy that fracture and fold the landscape.

Changing the landscape

As we can see from the picture below, earthquakes can cause dramatic movement on the earth's surface. This bridge was a straight, safe strip of road for years, until an earthquake ruptured and shifted the ground on which it stood. Strain and pressure may have been building up underground for a long time. When the pressure became too great, the earth shifted. This phenomenon is known as **offset** and can affect bridges and railroad tracks in the same way. The same movement also displaces rivers, so that they have to make a new **channel.** The lower parts of the rivers can be left with no direct source of water.

This road, which is offset, is now lying quite still. The road and the earth beneath it have shifted into a new position.

Earth tremors can also cause **subsidence,** when part of the ground suddenly sinks. Subsidence appears on the surface as a steep step in a rock, and it splits the level of roads, railroads, or bridges, making them impassable. If the ground beneath a river or stream subsides, the water will cascade steeply over the lip of the top half, making a waterfall or a rapid.

The diagram on page 12 showed an example of a **reverse fault.** Reverse faults are often associated with folded layers of rock. This type of fault does not always bring cracks to the surface. Instead, it can fold the ground above it into huge, wavy layers of rock. Both faults and folds are responses to forces pushing blocks or the earth's crust together, but folding can occur without faulting. The folds caused by reverse fault movement do have some advantages. On the edge of Coalinga, in California, a huge underground petroleum oil reservoir has been folded upwards over millions of years by the reverse fault line beneath it. When an earthquake struck in May 1983, the oil was brought close enough to the surface to be used.

As tremors split and crack the ground, they also break water pipes, flooding buildings and weakening their structure still further. When sewage pipes fracture, waste water mixes with clean water, making it unsafe to drink.

Tsunami!

The map on page 4 shows that many of the earth's major fault lines run along coastlines and across the ocean floor. This means that tremors often occur near water, or right underneath it. Some types of **seismic waves** can pass through water, so a shift in the surface of the ocean floor can have consequences far above.

Walls of water

A **tsunami** is a parade of high-energy waves, capable of rising very high and causing major damage. They are often called tidal waves, but this name is misleading— they have nothing to do with tides. Tsunamis are caused mostly by earthquakes, although sometimes volcanic activity under the ocean can cause them too. When the ocean floor is abruptly displaced, a swell of water makes waves across the surface. These become faster and more powerful as they travel, until they crash ashore. Across the deep Pacific Ocean these waves can travel at about 435 miles (700 kilometers) per hour. As they approach the coast and the ocean becomes shallower, the waves build up even higher and crash over onto the shore.

The enormous power of a tsunami can carry massive objects ashore and devastate the coast.

Wide, open, and deep shorelines usually suffer little from tsunamis. A wave will rise only very slightly, almost unseen. Buoys and small boats might rock gently, and sand and pebbles might be pushed a little way up the beach, but there will be no real danger from the wave.

On the other hand, curved, shallow bays concentrate the strength of the tsunami, making it squeeze into a smaller space. This boosts the height of the wave as it hits the shore. They can rise 100 feet (30 meters) high and can hit land at 160 miles (250 kilometers) per hour. People who are in the way are in danger of being completely swept away or dragged out to sea by the powerful undercurrent. Buildings are crushed, trees are snapped in half or uprooted, and boats are shattered into splinters.

In 1755, a great earthquake measuring about 8.5 on the **Richter scale** flattened Lisbon, the capital of Portugal. It was followed just 40 minutes later by a huge tsunami that was probably more than 50 feet (15 meters) high.

Pressure points

- Most tsunamis are caused by earthquakes with **foci** less than 30 miles (50 kilometers) below the ocean floor.

- Most tsunamis are caused by earthquakes above a **magnitude** of 6.5 on the Richter scale.

- The most deadly tsunamis have foci less than 16 miles (25 kilometers) below the surface of the ocean floor.

Rumbling and Erupting

The earth's crust rumbles and cracks as it slips and slides over the sticky **mantle** beneath. When parts of the mantle become molten because of the heat of the core, the **magma** can push up through weak points and **fissures** in the crust, making volcanoes. Some volcanoes form deep down on the ocean floor, while others rise above sea level, solidifying into islands. Over millions of years, many have made chains of mountains along the edges of continents. As the map shows, a lot of these run along the edges of **tectonic plates,** in exactly the same places as earthquake activity. Volcanic eruption is not always explosive. Sometimes magma moves slowly upwards and oozes out like molasses. As it travels up the **conduit,** this red-hot magma cracks the inside surface of the rock, causing tremors.

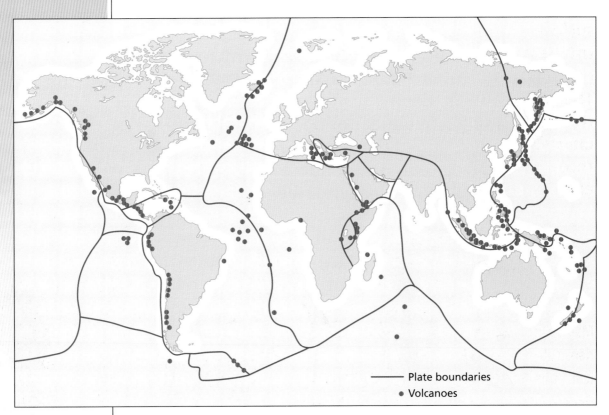

Plate boundaries
• Volcanoes

Although many volcanoes erupt along tectonic plate boundaries, others seem to pop out of the centers of plates in areas known as hotspots.

Tell-tale tremors

The ground around a volcano often rumbles for hours or even days before an eruption. **Vulcanologists** take a great interest in any earth tremors that occur on or around a resting volcano. In March 1980, in Washington state, Mount St. Helens awoke with a small eruption, after being **dormant** for 137 years. This was followed by two months of earth tremors that produced a 3-mile (5-kilometer) crack in the side of the volcano. They watched as magma slowly pushed out a bulge on the northeast slope. These studies enabled them to predict that Mount St. Helens would at some point soon produce a devastating eruption. In May 1980, Mount St. Helens erupted so fiercely that a huge hole was blasted in its northeast face.

A vulcanologist named Milton Garces is developing a new way of predicting volcanic eruptions. From the surface of the crater he measures changes in **infrasound**—minute wavelengths of sound that humans cannot hear. These vibrate right from the **magma chamber,** up through the conduit and into the **vent.**

Magma is hotter and less dense than solid rock, so it rises to the surface, finding its way through fissures, cracks, or weak points in the crust.

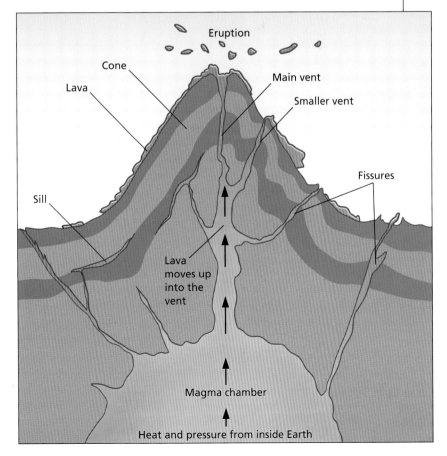

Eruption

Cone

Lava

Main vent

Smaller vent

Fissures

Sill

Lava moves up into the vent

Magma chamber

Heat and pressure from inside Earth

Measuring and Predicting
Mighty Measurements

How do we measure earthquakes? How do we know when "the big one" will strike? We can only really answer the first of these questions properly. Measuring the strength of earthquakes, finding their **epicenter,** and tracking their spread are all parts of the science of **seismology**—the study of seismic waves.

Pressure points

These are some of the instruments used to measure earthquakes.

- **Seismometer**—a very sensitive instrument that picks up the pattern of ground tremors and traces them on a paper roll or magnetic tape. The continual pattern makes a **seismograph.**

- Two kinds of seismometer use a swinging pendulum or an electromagnetic galvanometer, an instrument that measures **electromagnetic** currents, to pick up the tremors—even very slight ones.

- **Accelerometers** are instruments that only work when a tremor is huge. They are not sensitive to small movements, but they are much stronger than seismometers, which can be destroyed in a large earthquake.

This **seismologist** is reading a seismograph that is recording tremors registered by a seismometer. One of the problems of seismometers is that they must be very sensitive, but they also have to be able to withstand violent tremors.

The Richter scale

The earthquake measurements given in this book are all on the **Richter scale.** Invented by the American seismologist Dr. Charles Richter in 1935, it gives values for the amount of energy released by **seismic waves** that radiate from the **focus.** This is the **magnitude.** Each whole number on the scale is ten times more powerful than the one before it, and each can be linked to the amount of destruction it causes. By taking measurements at different stations, seismologists can trace them back and find the earthquake's origin.

Magnitude	Effect
1	Cannot be felt on the surface and can only be detected by instruments near the epicenter
2	Can be felt only slightly near the epicenter
3	Can be felt near the epicenter but causes little damage
4-5	Can be felt at a distance of about 20 miles (30 kilometers) from the epicenter and can cause some damage in small areas
6	Can be clearly felt over a wide area and can cause a fair amount of damage
7	Buildings fall, people are killed, and damaging **tsunamis** can be generated
8	Widespread destruction, possibly including tsunami disaster, will occur

It is very difficult to describe exactly what will happen when an earthquake of a particular magnitude strikes. Buildings that are specially built to withstand earthquakes will not fall as easily as those that are built in the conventional way.

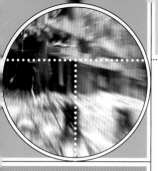

More Measurements

Other scales were developed as scientists realized that, however much shaking and rumbling took place, it was the amount of displacement along the fracture that mattered most. A small displacement would generally cause less damage than a large one. The impact on humans also depends on what they have built on top of the fracture.

Measuring the damage

Some scales include not only seismic measurements, but also what people can actually feel and see during an earthquake. This can be very useful if it is compared with the other scales and linked to the type of ground and structures built on it. It helps to predict what might happen during an earthquake of a particular size in a particular place, even if it isn't useful for earthquake prediction itself.

In 1966, the Japanese seismologist Kei Aki created a measuring system based on **seismic motion.** This calculation included not just surface movement and damage but also the duration of the tremor—how long it lasts—and the amount of fault movement.

Probably the best scale of this type was developed by Giuseppe Mercalli in 1902. He established twelve different grades of damage to buildings, roads, and other structures. Over the next 30 years, these scales went out of date. More electric cables, telegraph lines, and power stations had been built, the automobile and bus had replaced the horse and carriage, and more roads and bridges had been made to carry them. Two other scientists, Wood and Neumann, helped to revise the scale, which is now known as the Mercalli-Wood-Neumann scale. It is one of the most trusted measurements of surface damage and is still widely used today.

Pressure points

This is Grade 8 on the Mercalli-Wood-Neumann scale, and shows some of the kinds of things that are considered.

"Damage is slight in specially designed structures; considerable in ordinary, substantial buildings, with partial collapse; great in poorly-built structures....Fall of chimneys, factory stacks, columns, monuments...Heavy furniture overturned....Changes in water levels in wells. Earthquake disturbs persons who are driving motor cars."

A worldwide web

Computers are now used to analyze data collected by more traditional earthquake-measuring devices such as **seismometers.** Computer technology is also being linked to satellite communications to create a worldwide earthquake study system. This is focused on stations in three earthquake zones— Africa, Antarctica, and South America. The system is called the **Global Telemetered Seismograph Network.**

One of the biggest earthquakes ever, measuring 8.4 on the **Richter scale,** shattered the city of Anchorage, Alaska in 1964, causing massive landslides and a **tsunami** that reached as far as the Californian coast.

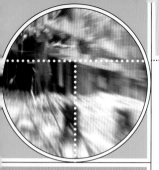

Seeking Tsunamis

The tremors of a **magnitude** 8 earthquake in the middle of an ocean might not affect anyone living on land directly, but they could cause a huge **tsunami.** Tsunamis are silent until they strike. Without monitoring and warning systems, they can take people completely by surprise. The most vulnerable communities live on small islands, especially those in the Pacific Ocean, which do not have the resources to protect themselves.

A center for tsunami-spotting

In the United States, half a million people live in the path of tsunamis reaching 50 feet (15 meters) high, while over a million are at risk of suffering tsunamis towering over 100 feet (30 meters). Most of these occur in the Hawaiian Islands, which have been battered by over 170 tsunamis in the last 200 years— that's almost one every year!

Pressure points

Japan has spent much time and money developing ways to prevent tsunami disaster. Some of the steps they have taken include:

- building **breakwaters** and zigzag concrete sea-walls—concrete barriers that break the waves as they hit the shore
- building seafront hotels on concrete stilts so that water rushes between the pillars and underneath the hotel rooms
- moving homes, shops, and offices inland—away from danger
- building several roads leading inland from the shore. This ensures that people can escape easily and quickly, without panic and accidents, when a tsunami warning is given.

Hawaii is a real hotspot. Not only do its own earthquakes and volcanoes make their own tsunamis, but it also lies in the path of tsunamis generated far away across the sea. Because Hawaii lies at the heart of tsunami action, in 1946 the National Oceanographic and Atmospheric Administration (NOAA) chose to set up the **Pacific Tsunami Warning System** (PTWS) in Hawaii. Seismic and tide stations monitor the Pacific Basin from all the major harbors in the region.

Hawaii's sophisticated tsunami warning system alerts people to even the smallest risk—but they do not always pay attention. Some people have been **evacuated** from a beach only to find out later that the tsunami was tiny. People stop worrying about warnings and are more reluctant to hurry away from a danger spot.

Tools of the trade

The main instruments used to detect and measure tsunami waves are the **seismograph,** which detects earth movement that may start a tsunami wave, and the **tide gauge,** which measures the height of the ocean surface. A tide gauge is a float set in a vertical tank of water in a sheltered area like a harbor. The float rises and falls with the water. A measuring instrument is attached to the float and records its movement. Tide gauges are not intended to predict incoming tsunamis, but to tell when a tsunami is moving out towards other harbors. Computers are now used to collect all these statistics and build up a picture of how waves behave and what impact they will have.

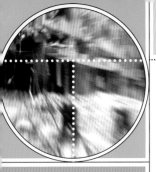

Imperfect Predictions

All the statistics gathered on earthquakes throughout the world have not yet led to a major breakthrough in earthquake prediction. Through careful monitoring, **seismologists** can tell when stresses are building in a particular area or section of an existing fault. This tells them that a big release of pressure—an earthquake—will happen soon, but in earthquake terms, "soon" can mean 50 years!

So many people live in earthquakes zones that **evacuation** is pointless without accurate earthquake prediction. In San Francisco or Los Angeles, for example, millions of people would have to leave their homes in order to get out of the range of a large earthquake. An evacuation that large would be very expensive, and it could be years before the earthquake actually hit!

The Parkfield experiment

Parkfield is a town in California that experiences a large earthquake roughly every 22 years. Seismologists believe that the origin and track of the quakes is always more or less the same. An earthquake was expected to hit Parkfield just before 1993, so scientists from the U.S. Geological Survey visited the site and drilled holes deep down into the crust. Here they placed **seismometers,** while on the surface they set up lasers that projected beams from one building to another. This was to measure any movement of the buildings and therefore any shift in the ground. These and other instruments worked around the clock, watching for the earthquake. The scientists waited eagerly. At last they were in a position to track an earthquake from its beginning to its end. 1993 came and went—so did 1994—and no earthquake struck. They are still waiting!

Making maps

We can tell how much **tectonic plates** are shifting past each other, but there are always areas along the fault zone that become stuck for some time before finally shifting. The portions of a fault zone that have not had any recent seismic activity are known as **seismic gaps.** Seismologists expect strain to be building along these gaps, so fault rupture is expected there in the future.

This prediction method is not very accurate—it cannot pinpoint exactly when an earthquake will occur. It also only applies to quakes along the edges of tectonic plates, and the method tends to divert attention from other areas at risk. In Japan in the 1970s, all eyes were on the Tokai area south of Tokyo, which was thought to be nearing the end of its seismic cycle—a big quake might soon occur. Instead, an earthquake occurred along a different portion of the fault zone, hitting the other side of Japan and killing 106 people.

This colored satellite radar image shows the Hector Mine earthquake on October 16, 1999 in California. The colored bands show displacement of ground, with the tightest bands at the **epicenter.** This earthquake measured 7.1 on the **Richter scale.**

Other Methods

A huge quake struck the Japanese city of Kobe in 1965—400 years after the last major quake, which was recorded by Buddhist monks. Over 6,000 people died in this earthquake and, ever since, predicting the next one has been a top priority. But while Japan has the most expensive and up-to-date earthquake prediction systems in the world, they—like everyone else—have yet to predict a major earthquake accurately!

Strange changes

In Kobe, prediction tools include satellite images, which are supposed to show movements in the earth's crust. Ten days before the next major earthquake struck in 1995, these tools failed to show any changes, although during this time, strange changes were seen in the sky, which turned from red to green to blue. The people of Kobe reported that they noticed unusual things happening in their homes, too. The hands of electric clocks dropped down towards the 6. Air conditioners began to stop and start on their own. Television channels switched from one to another without so much as a button being pressed. At night, the moon appeared to some to have a pinkish hue.

After ten days the quake struck. No one had been **evacuated** because the scientific instruments had not indicated that an earthquake was imminent. Afterwards, scientists began to analyze the strange stories that had flooded in over the past few days. Many believe that changes in the earth's **electromagnetism** may have caused some of these phenomena. They linked it to observations made some way away in the city of Kyoto, which had experienced severe electric storms with blinding lightning. So what should we trust—our instruments or our eyes?

Sensitive creatures

In China one ancient method that is still used to predict earthquakes is the study of animal behavior. This method has been dismissed by scientists in some other parts of the world, but in February 1975, in Haicheng, **hibernating** snakes rose from their nests in the middle of winter. **Seismologists** used this information, together with other statistics, to predict an earthquake successfully. Haicheng was evacuated and hundreds of thousands of lives were saved.

Human instinct

Some people living in earthquake zones believe that symptoms such as sickness, dizziness, headaches, and heart palpitations are all indications that the earth is about to crack. It would be easy to dismiss these claims but, as we have seen, changes in electrical and magnetic forces as well as deep stirrings in the earth's crust affect the delicate instruments that scientists have created. Our bodies, too, are delicate instruments. Can they also detect the changes?

Some scientists use **hot springs** to help them predict earthquakes. Some **geysers**, such as Old Faithful in Yellowstone Park, erupt very regularly. When their pattern changes, it is an early signal that the earth underneath may be moving.

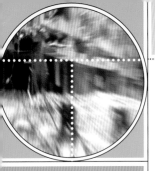

Getting out of the Way

There is no way of preventing earthquakes. Predicting them is not an exact science as yet. Fleeing from them is virtually impossible. So is it possible to warn people?

A ray of hope

A new warning system developed along the San Andreas Fault in California is helping people to get out of the way. The warnings do not give enough time for people to escape from the area, but they do give a chance to get out of a building that could crumble or catch fire. When fast, strong tremors are picked up, an automatic warning light flashes in earthquake centers around the region.

Tremors can travel as fast as 4.4 miles (7 kilometers) per second—faster than the speed of sound. Slower tremors can travel at about 2 miles (3.2 kilometers) per second. This gives people living 100 miles (160 kilometers) away from the **epicenter** between 20 and 50 seconds to get out of the way, if they are warned in time. In 1994, in Mexico City, this was enough to **evacuate** many people from city center buildings successfully.

The worst effects of earthquakes upon people are fire and falling buildings, as in the San Francisco earthquake of 1989. It is vital that the fire service is able to function quickly and efficiently.

Weary of warnings?

Every year there are about 30,000 tremors in California alone. In June 1988, a **magnitude** 5 tremor hit an area about 50 miles (80 kilometers) from San Francisco. A public warning was issued because it was thought that an even bigger tremor would soon strike. What were people supposed to do? No one knew whether a big earthquake would strike within days or even months. Life, work—and even school—must go on! Early in 1989 another public warning was given. A few months later, San Francisco was struck by a magnitude 7.1 earthquake. No one could have been prepared for the exact moment at which it struck. No one could have moved away from the city for a whole year, just waiting for it!

Pressure points

As we have seen, **tsunamis** can follow earth tremors. They move more slowly, which makes them easier to predict and track. This also makes warnings and evacuations easier.

- It takes three hours to evacuate a city the size of Honolulu, Hawaii, so tsunami warnings have to be made well in advance.

- It costs $30 million to evacuate a city the size of Honolulu. This makes false alarms very expensive.

- In California, computer models have predicted that a large earth tremor on the Santa Catarina fault line will cause a dangerous **tsunami** eight minutes later. It will probably strike just north of Los Angeles International airport.

- Scientists from the University of California want **hazard maps** to be published in all telephone directories. If a tsunami strikes, this will enable people to fir   safe place well out of the path of the waves.

Why Live in Danger?

Thirty percent of the world's largest and fastest-growing cities lie in the most dangerous earthquake zones. That means a total of 600 million people are living in the way of earthquakes. The map on page 4 shows that earthquake zones cover a huge part of the earth's surface. Many of these zones are strung along the coastlines of continents where fishing communities have grown, and port cities have developed crucial trade links with the rest of the world.

In the Mediterranean region, ancient cities show how civilizations grew up along important trade routes. These ran from the Far East to the west of Europe, and right across the Sahara into West Africa. Such cities developed because they were quite simply in the most advantageous places to live—the threat of earthquakes was a small consideration. Even areas known to lie on a fault may only experience large quakes every several hundred years. A disaster may not strike for generations.

The hilltop village of Calabritto in southern Italy was struck by an earthquake on November 23, 1980. A lot of damage happened when rubble cascaded from the top, damaging the homes beneath.

Rural rumblings

Earthquakes obviously cause a lot of deaths in cities, where there are high concentrations of people. In more rural areas, whole towns and villages can be totally wiped out. The people living in them are usually farming communities. It would be far too difficult for them to uproot themselves and find new land in a safer place. In the southern Mediterranean region especially, getting out of harm's way is not an option, as so much of the area lies in a danger zone. In 1908, the Sicilian town of Messina and the surrounding countryside were struck by an earthquake that measured about 7.5 on the **Richter scale.** Small towns and villages were totally flattened, and 58,000 people died. On top of this tragedy, the agricultural economy was wrecked, with few people left to revitalize it.

Where next?

It isn't always obvious where the next big earthquake will strike. For example, the American midwest does not lie on any **tectonic plate** boundaries, but geologists have found over 100 fault lines. One of these, the New Madrid fault, caused a series of earthquakes in 1811 and 1812, including one of the strongest the U.S. has ever seen. There has not been a serious earthquake in this region since then, but there have been several thousand smaller tremors. **Seismologists** believe that a widespread quake of at least **magnitude** 7 on the Richter scale is likely to strike within the next 50 years. The Midwest is farming country, but there are also several major cities in the region, such as Memphis and St. Louis. If a large earthquake did strike, it would be disastrous for both humans and agriculture. However, another hundred years could pass without any major problems.

Rescue from the Rubble

Shattered services

Many victims of earthquake disasters are rescued by search teams from other countries, using trained sniffer dogs and heat-sensitive equipment to locate people buried under the rubble. Outside help is needed because local transport, **communications,** and emergency services have usually been severely damaged.

Burst water pipes prevent water from being pumped up to put out fires. Fractured gas pipes and ruptured electricity cables can cause widespread fires. If many separate fires grow uncontrolled, they can explode into firestorms. In these situations, flames roar upwards, sucking in air underneath, fanning them in searing-hot winds that can reach speeds of 100 miles (160 kilometers) per hour. Other problems facing rescue teams and aid agencies include **aftershocks,** disease brought about by contaminated water supplies, and lack of shelter.

Earthquake education

Panic kills. Japan has recognized that its people need to know what to do in an earthquake, so that orderly **evacuation** can take place. In earthquake training centers, people are taught what to do if an earthquake strikes. Some are placed in a room set on a moving floor. The floor shakes to simulate tremors, furniture slides about, and dishes crash to the floor. People are trained to turn off the gas flame on the stove, switch off electrical appliances, put on special helmets and masks, and then to crawl under the table. In addition, towns, villages, and cities all over Japan hold an earthquake preparation day each year, which includes first aid courses.

Pressure points

The problems below that faced Armenia after the December 1988 earthquake show just how difficult it is for poorer nations to cope. Over 700,000 people in all were affected by the earthquake, including 100,000 who were killed.

- Many of the buildings in Armenia were poorly constructed from concrete that tends to crumble. Many more buildings fell than would normally be expected in an earthquake-ready city from an earthquake measuring 6.9 on the **Richter scale.**

- Rescue attempts were made difficult by poor transport and communications.

- International search teams, with special tracing equipment and dogs, did not arrive until two days after the quake. Until this time, only untrained rescuers tried to find survivors.

- Hospitals had been damaged and medical staff killed.

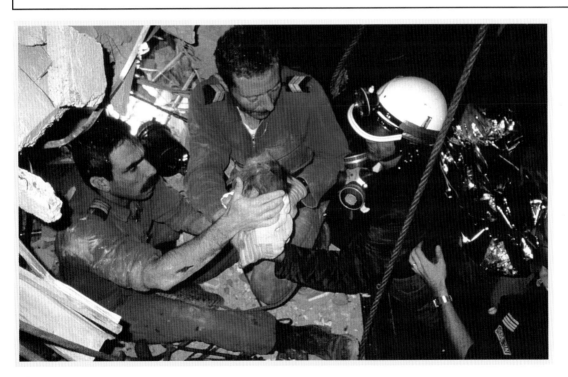

This is all that is left of a hospital that collapsed during the Mexico City earthquake disaster of 1985. But among the rubble, a whole week after the catastrophe, newborn babies were being pulled out alive.

Design for Survival

One of the most important ways in which we can improve the chances of survival in a serious earthquake is to make sure our buildings remain standing.

Better buildings

Architects, engineers, and builders have been building with earthquakes in mind for several centuries. After the earthquake in Turkey in 1509, the government invested a lot of money to ensure that all mosques were built with reinforced arches and strengthened curved ceilings and domes.

However, even today, in many parts of the Middle East and the Mediterranean, houses are often built of thick, heavy stone or earthen walls, with roofs supported by large beams. The thick walls might seem very protective, but they are not strengthened by supports and can still collapse in an earthquake. However, traditional houses in villages in southern Portugal have two interesting features. First, the outer surfaces of the thick walls slant inward. This helps prop up the inner section. The other feature is the roof, which is lined with lightweight bamboo canes and poles that would not be too destructive if they fell.

This elegant building in Lisbon's Praca do Comercio was built immediately after the devastating earthquake of 1755. It was built with fire-resistant partitions and reinforced walls.

Modern methods

Nowadays, architects and engineers in earthquake zones make shock-resistance a priority. Some tall buildings are set on floating bases that absorb the energy of a tremor. Electronically-controlled **counterweights** are attached to the top. These rock away from the direction of the shake, keeping the building from swaying. Other buildings are set on rubber or steel pads, raising them from ground. This helps them to cope when the ground is pulled sideways. Special building materials, including metals and concrete, are created to absorb shocks. New types of shatter-resistant glass are being developed.

Inside, large buildings also have to be designed so that there are enough clear exits and fire escapes. In Los Angeles, equipment has been developed for making sure that furniture and fittings stay in place when the room shakes.

One of the most important considerations is the land on which buildings are constructed. This must not be too soft and loose, or it may lead to **liquefaction.** It also must not lie on top of hidden faults.

There was massive damage to the Kiteko Dam Complex in Kobe, Japan during the earthquake in 1995.

Shaking Nature

Harming homes and habitats

When the earth shakes, it can take the lives of plants and animals and alter the face of their natural habitats. Birds' nests, wasps' nests, beehives, rabbit warrens, badger dens, beaver lodges—all these can be destroyed when an earthquake shakes the land. Adults and young can be buried, or the mating and nest-building season may be disturbed. Animals can be forced out of **hibernation** in cold weather, before food is available for them to eat. Creatures that **estivate** are forced to the surface, where the temperatures are too extreme for them to survive.

During an earthquake, the land surface can be broken up or covered by landslides. Severe and prolonged shaking uproots trees and bushes. During the New Madrid earthquakes of 1811 and 1812, three tremors reached over 8 on the **Richter scale.** Many trees toppled over as their roots loosened in the soil. Massive land **subsidence** and uplift ripped apart rivers and streams, leaving aquatic plants and animals high and dry. The quakes were so strong that the Mississippi River temporarily flowed the wrong way, and its course was permanently changed!

These delicate sea creatures need seawater to wash over them regularly. In 1822, a huge earthquake along the coast of Chile thrust a section of the seashore upwards by over 3 feet (1 meter), exposing beds of shellfish and seaweeds. They all dried out in the sun.

Tall stories?

We know that animals seem to sense earthquakes. There are many more strange tales reported—of catfish that dance around wildly, of rats that rush up to attics a week before an earthquake, and of stray cats that just disappear off the streets. An hour before the 1989 San Francisco earthquake, pigeons were too nervous to leave their coops.

These stories might seem doubtful, but researchers have found that it may be possible for animals to sense quakes. It has been discovered that bees are deeply disturbed by the moving forces under the ground. This may be because of the **magnetite** in their bodies. In normal circumstances this helps them to find their location, but it also reacts strongly to **electromagnetic** waves. Honeybees are especially sensitive. All animals have certain levels of magnetite, and so do we!

A **tsunami** can can cover a beach with sand, mud, and other debris, as well as completely destroying animal life and natural habitats. This is a beach near Miami, Florida, after a tsunami.

Earthquakes in History

Where's the evidence?

All over the world there is evidence of ancient earthquakes—huge land-slips, faults, and thrusted blocks scar the landscape, while folded mountains bear witness to the churning earth.

Geologists can determine how once-flat, continuous layers of rock have been folded and displaced by tectonic activity. **Radiocarbon dating** can reveal if remains of ancient vegetation on a lower piece of land once grew on a level with rock that now towers above. Scientists look for traces of a form of carbon called "carbon 14" in decayed or fossilized plants that they find in both the lower and upper parts of slipped land. The carbon breaks down at a known rate, so by measuring the amount of carbon 14 still in the plant matter, scientists can find out how long ago the plants were alive. Sometimes scientists may also find the same animal and plant fossils on different land levels, which shows that at one time the surface was flat.

Seismologists in history

It has taken a long time for scientists to discover how earthquakes happen, and they still do not know everything. The **plate tectonics theory** became widely accepted only 30 years ago, but the mystery of earthquakes has puzzled scientists since ancient times. The Greek philosopher and scientist Aristotle believed that earthquakes were caused by trapped air exploding from beneath the ground. Modern theories only emerged after the development of instruments that could measure sound waves under the earth's surface. One of the first was made in 1883 by John Milne, an English mechanical engineer and geologist. It was a **seismograph** powered by clockwork.

Pressure points

- Deposits in the mudflats of Washington state reveal that the area was once swamped by a massive **tsunami.**

- An 8-inch (20-centimeter) sand deposit was dumped by a tsunami several miles inland from the Scottish coast of Montrose 7,000 years ago. The deposits were discovered in 1974 by students from Coventry University in England.

- Chunks of land snapped off the Hawaiian Islands, probably over 100,000 years ago. This may have caused tsunami waves 1,000 feet (300 meters) high as far away as Australia, Japan, or the United States.

Over the next 70 years, using a network of seismic instruments, an accurate world map of active fault lines was drawn. It was remarkably similar to one constructed by an Irish civil engineer, Robert Mallet, in 1857, without using any instruments. He had mapped all the earthquake evidence available to him through geological studies and eyewitness accounts. Although his map is incomplete, it is very much like modern fault line maps. His studies helped future researchers to discover that most earth tremors occur along **tectonic plates.**

These are the earthquake-shattered ruins of the Temple of Apollo in Corinth, Greece. All around the Mediterranean and Middle East, crumbled ancient cities are evidence of devastating earthquake activity.

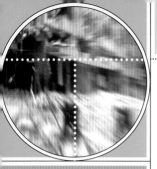

Earth-shattering Earthquakes

Top ten most deadly earthquakes

Earthquakes have many different effects. It is impossible to estimate the strength of early earthquakes, and difficult to count how many people have been killed by them. No list can be truly accurate.

Location of earthquake	Date	Number of people killed
Damghan, Iran	December 22, 856	200,000
Ardabil, Iran	March 23, 893	150,000
Aleppo, Syria	August 9, 1138	230,000
Chihli, China	September 1290	100,000
Shanshi, China	Jan 23, 1556	830,000
Calcutta, India	Oct 11, 1737	300,000
Gansu, China	December 16, 1920	200,000
Kanto Plain, Japan	September 1, 1923	142,800
Nan-Shan, China	May 22, 1927	200,000
Tangshan, China	July 27, 1976	242,000

Pressure points

- Two million people were killed by earthquakes in the 20th century alone, but in total, there was only one hour of major earthquake shaking.

- There can be millions of earthquakes every year worldwide, but only a small number (about 120) will cause destruction. Hundreds will cause minor damage.

- The largest earthquake recorded reached 9.5 on the **Richter scale** in Chile on May 2, 1960. Many cities were badly damaged, landslides occurred in many places, and an area of land 530 miles (850 kilometers) long and 80 miles (130 kilometers) wide was displaced by the fault.

In October 1997, a series of earthquakes hit the town of Assisi in Italy, and the 700-year-old church was slightly damaged. It contains precious wall paintings, or frescoes, created by a famous artist named Giotto. While people were examining the damage, a huge **aftershock** struck the basilica. Four people died, and the frescoes were shattered. The photo on the left shows the moment of collapse. The tiny pieces were gathered together, and the works have been restored.

Glossary

accelerometer   device that measures tremors that are so huge they would destroy a seismometer

aftershock   minor earthquake that follows a stonger one

amplitude   height of a wave

body wave   group of seismic waves that move through solid rock

breakwater   concrete barrier built near the coast to break up large, destructive waves before they can cause damage on the shore

channel   course carved into rock by a river or stream

communications   facilities like roads, railroads, and telephone lines

conduit   channel that leads from a volcano's magma chamber to its vent

counterweight   weight used to balance out the weight of an object

electromagnetism   magnetic force caused by an electric current

epicenter   point on the earth's surface that lies directly above the focus of an earthquake

estivate   to slow down body processes and sleep through the summer

evacuate   to move people to safety

fault creep   slow, non-quaking movements of sections of the earth's crust

fissure   crack in rock or the earth's crust

focus   (plural is foci) point where an earthquake originates

frequency   number of waves passing a fixed point within a certain time

geologist   scientist who studies the earth and earth processes

geyser   hot water spout, like a fountain, that spurts up from volcanically heated rock beneath the earth's surface

Global Telemetered Seismograph Network   computerized satellite-linked worldwide earthquake monitoring system

granite   hard rock with a uniform texture that makes up large portions of continental crust

hazard map   map showing the areas most likely to experience earthquake disaster

hibernate   to slow down body processes and sleep through the winter

hot spring   spring of water heated by hot volcanic rock beneath the earth's surface

infrasound   very small wavelengths of sound that humans cannot hear

infrastructure   means of transportation, communication, and services, such as roads, railroads, electricity, and sewers

insurance policy   promise by an insurance company to pay for damage caused to property by a disaster. The owner of the property must make regular payments to the insurance company.

interference   the effect two waves have on each other

lava   hot molten rock that oozes or flows above the earth's surface

liquefaction   phenomenon that occurs when a tremor shakes soft or loose rock so much that it moves around like a liquid

magma   hot molten rock below the earth's surface

magma chamber   well of magma that seeps up into the earth's crust

magnetite   magnetic iron oxide

magnitude   measure of energy released by seismic waves that radiate from the focus of an earthquake, based on seismometer readings

mantle   hot layer of rock that surrounds the earth's crust

offset dramatic sideways or up-and-down movement on the earth's surface

Pacific Tsunami Warning System (PTWS) earthquake monitoring system that predicts tsunami waves anywhere within the Pacific Basin

plate tectonics theory set of ideas about how shifting tectonic plates have formed the earth as it is today

pressure wave type of body wave that vibrates lengthwise, in the same direction as the wave is traveling

radiocarbon dating method of finding out how old plant or animal material is by measuring the deterioration of a special form of carbon

reverse fault backward-sloping fault that forms in land masses that have been compressed

Richter Scale scale that gives values for the amount of energy released by seismic waves. It was invented by Dr. Charles Richter in 1935.

sediment soft rock or soil particles often deposited by water or wind

seismic gap portion of an active fault that has not had any seismic activity for a long time, suggesting a build-up of stress

seismic motion vibrations of the earth associated with earthquakes

seismic wave wave of energy that travels through the earth

seismograph instrument that traces the pattern of ground tremors onto a paper roll or a magnetic tape. The pattern is registered by a seismometer.

seismologist scientist who studies movements in the earth's crust

seismology study of movements in the earth's crust

seismometer instrument that picks up the pattern of ground tremors

shear wave body wave that vibrates at right angles to the direction it is traveling

subduction zone place where one tectonic plate slips down beneath another plate

subsidence when a section of the earth sinks

surface wave group of energy waves that move along bands or layers of rock

tectonic plate huge slab of the earth's crust. The plates move apart and together, sometimes rubbing against each other.

tide gauge instrument that measures local changes in the height of the ocean

tsunami series of fast-moving ocean waves caused by earthquakes, volcanic activity, or any sudden movement of the sea floor

vent opening inside a volcano through which the magma erupts

vulcanologist scientist who studies volcanic activity

More Books to Read

Bennett, Paul. *Earthquake.* North Manako, Minn.: Smart Apple Media, 1999.

Martin, Fred. *Earthquakes.* Chicago: Heinemann Library, 1998.

Meister, Cari. *Earthquakes.* Minneapolis, Minn.: ABDO Publishing Co., 1999.

Index